Divorce

The Ultimate Guide on How to Get over a Divorce and Feel Happy Again

Linda Stark

Adherence to all applicable laws and regulations, including international, federal, state, and local governing professional licensing, business practices, advertising, and all other aspects of doing business in the US, Canada, or any other jurisdiction is the sole responsibility of the purchaser or reader.

Neither the author nor the publisher assumes any responsibility or liability whatsoever on the behalf of the purchaser or reader of these materials.

Any perceived slight of any individual or organization is purely unintentional.

Table of Contents

Linda Stark

Introduction

Hello, my name is Linda Stark and I want to thank you for downloading my book.

Divorce is never fun or easy; but you are taking the first step towards a new and better life when you realize that you have the power to make it through. You will be able to survive this truly difficult phase. After your divorce is final, you will have a new chance to thrive and live your life with love, happiness and abundance.

This book contains proven steps and strategies on how to live through the difficult process of divorce and recovery. You will learn the different stages of divorce so you can better prepare yourself in handling all the negative emotions that you will struggle with. You will also learn how to look at the brighter perspective of divorce to help you let go of the past and move towards a better future. The book aims to help you learn how to forgive other people and more importantly, yourself so you can focus your attention to better taking care of yourself and finding new meaning in your life. I truly hope that you will soon be able to start living the loving, happy and abundant life that you deserve.

Chapter 1

Stages of Divorce

In our modern society, divorce has become one of those emotional tasks that people normally go through. Different people go through divorce in various ways. There are some people who experience all of the extreme emotional stages discussed below while other people go through divorce more easily as they are more skilled in maneuvering through difficult stages. here is what you should keep in mind: all of the emotions you will read below are normal. You may find that you can easily acknowledge some of these emotions while you may also be inclined to become more uncomfortable admitting that you feel some of the other emotions.

It is very important that you learn how to recognize and acknowledge your emotions, especially those that you will go through during the early phases of your divorce they can greatly diminish your capability to think clearly which can eventually lead you to make rash and impaired judgments. There will be days when making rational decisions can be quite difficult or even impossible. you have to constantly remind yourself that you need to control your own emotions before they start controlling you. It may seem like you have hit rock bottom and you can't see any hope for a better future; but you need to find even the slightest hope that after all the pain is gone, you will be able to start over again.

Sorrow and Grief

Experiencing sadness when your marriage is about to end is but natural. Even though this stage is painful, you need to realize that grief is really a healthy way to respond after losing a significant relationship. We are all meant to experience grief and it would not be sensible for you not to expect it. On some days, you may even feel like it is so difficult to handle grief and sadness. Understanding and accepting the certainty of these emotions can help you deal with them better.

The personal experiences of thousands of divorced people, a lot of theoretical writings and research studies have shown that the emotional effects that you experience during a divorce is comparable to the effects of having an immediate family die. The good news is that process of grief and recovery has its beginning, middle and end. If you are currently in the beginning or the middle stage, you may feel like all the confusion and pains seem endless. However, you can hold on to the truth that the confusion and pain will slowly lighten and eventually disappear.

It is important that you do not compare your own recovery process with other people. Some people may complete the process within a year but for others, it can last for several years. Allow yourself to go through the process based on your own pace.

It was Elisabeth Kübler-Ross, one of the forerunners in the hospice movement, who originally defined the five stages of grief from a significant trauma like divorce or death: denial, anger & resentment, bargaining, depression, and acceptance. When you are in the denial stage, you may constantly think that the divorce could not really be happening to you and your family. You may try to convince yourself that you and your spouse are just going through a misunderstanding or a midlife crisis. You try to convince yourself that you can still work things out.

Then, you will enter the anger and resentment stage when you realize that things will not work out. You will feel angry and blame your spouse for hurting you and allowing you to go through such pain. You will feel that your spouse and life, in general, is unfair to you and that you do not deserve whatever pain and anguish you are feeling. Then, the bargaining stage will begin. You will try to negotiate and use statements such as "If I agree to do whatever you want, can we get back together?" or "If you will stay, I promise I will change."

When your spouse turns all your offers down, you will start to move to the depression stage. You will eventually realize that your worst fears are actually happening, and things are beyond your control now. You will feel like all the pain that you are going through is too much for you to bear. You may even think of ruining the rest of your life or even ending it because you see no more value in it. Be prepared to acknowledge these thoughts and remind yourself that you are just going through the desperation stage. Allow yourself to grieve. When you are ready, you will ultimately reach the acceptance stage where you will finally admit that your divorce is final. It is up to you now to wallow in the past or to accept it and move on to a better future.

It is very important that you understand the above five stages as you talk about your divorce and make critical decisions. It is vital that you become fully aware when you are going through the first four stages of grief because it will be very hard for you to make sound decisions or even think clearly. When you are able to identify the stage of grief you are currently in, you will not only be able to determine the right steps you need to take to move forward but you will also be able to ask for the right help from the people you trust and love.

Guilt and Shame

When a person's marriage ends, going through shame and guilt is a normal reaction. Almost all of us feel these emotions when we feel a sense of failure. We feel guilty and ashamed for not being able to fulfill our own expectations or what we believe our community expects from us. Divorced people can feel ashamed or guilty for not being able to sustain their marriage. We can say that these emotions are rooted on both our personal expectations and what we perceive our culture expects from us. You may feel guilty for not being able to fulfill the promises that you have made to your spouse during your wedding day. You may feel ashamed and think that other people are saying negative things about you for having a failed marriage.

In order for you to overcome the feelings of guilt and shame, it is important that you first discern whether the expectations of your community about marriage and divorce are valid and realistic. If you look around you, is everyone really living those expectations? If the reality of marriage and divorce in your community does not match what you perceive the community expects from you, you may find it harder to overcome your shame and guilt. You will find it hard to clearly see reality as it is, acknowledge reality for what it is and handle all the problems and issues that come with divorce. Furthermore, it is now very common to hear about one or both spouses engaging in extreme deceit, betrayal or even criminal behavior that can heighten a spouse's feelings of shame and guilt.

Whether your feelings of guilt and shame are the result of not having met your own or the community's expectations or from an actual transgression, the feelings of shame and guilt can be so heartbreaking that they can rapidly transform into other emotions that seem more tolerable to endure like depression or anger. Sometimes, you jump to anger and depression without even realizing that shame and guilt have always been there. This is the reason why it is very common to see divorced people blaming each other. Sometimes, it can really be hard for divorcing spouses to accept that they are partly responsible for the failure of their marriage.

There are really only a few divorcing people who are very skilled in seeing or accepting their own feelings of shame and guilt. Normally, these negative and powerful emotions stay under the radar – invisible and hidden while doing the most pain and harm to you. When you have strong feelings of shame or guilt, you will find it hard or even not possible to maintain your perspective, accept more balanced information and to realistically ponder on your best options in resolving your issues and problems.

When you are guilty, you may start feeling like you have no right to ask for what you truly need in your divorce. This can lead to unbalanced negotiations and unrealistic settlements that you can regret in the future. You may have heard the adage "guilt has a short half-life". Since guilt is truly a difficult emotion, you can be easily tempted to transform it into anger. You may have heard of people who entered into agreements that are driven by guilt only to end up doubting themselves and returning to court to attempt to shake off impulsive settlements.

In the same way, your shame can also be transformed into rage, anger or blame directed at your husband or wife. These emotions can drive bitter fights between you and your spouse over property or children. At some point, you will be tempted to redirect your anger, which has to go somewhere, into disagreements and fights over issues that courts are allowed to decide on.

Anxiety and Fear

Humans have an innate instinct to "fight or take flight" which brings about our feelings of anxiety and fear. Your body reacts to stress stimuli (like an irate phone call from your wife) through your own physical alarm mechanisms. These are basically the same alarm mechanisms that enabled our ancestors to instantaneously react to bears and saber-toothed tigers. We can say that your body typically reacts to stress stimuli in the following ways:

You will first feel your heart speeding as adrenaline starts to pour into your bloodstream. With increased adrenaline level, you heart will start contracting more vigorously which can sometimes lead to a throbbing sensation in the head. You will start feeling hot flashes of energy as you focus your attention on the thing, person or situation that prompted the strong emotions. This will basically limit your capability to absorb new information. When you experience severe and chronic stress, you may end up having anxiety attacks which will cause you to tremble and your heart to pound.

It is even possible that you become paralyzed by your overpowering emotions of fear that seem to surface out of nowhere. All these emotions are commonly experienced by people who are nearing the end of their marriages. When you feel confused or dumbfounded in the same way, you may have the tendency to withdraw to your old habits of actions and thoughts instead of sharply scrutinizing all the facts that surround your situation and evaluating the best options for your future.

Old arguments will start to resurface.

As your marriage becomes unsettled and problematic, it is expected that you and your spouse will start relying on old habits of managing your differences that typically result in fights and disagreements instead of solutions. If your old habits did not help you in coming up with positive solutions during your marriage, you cannot really expect them to result in better outcomes during your divorce. Furthermore, if your spouse feels fearful and anxious about the situation, he or she may defy you and prevent you from moving forward and resolving all issues related to your divorce. This can happen while you start becoming impatient and finding no valid reasons for your divorce not to be over as soon as possible. These differences normally lead to bitter fights in the divorce court.

The sad news is that both our culture and our court system urge people to make decisions about their divorces based on how they feel while being stuck at the bottom of their emotional roller coaster ride. They have to make almost permanent decisions when they are most gripped by shame, guilt, grief, fear and anxiety. In any case, this is also the time when people are typically motivated to first contact their divorce lawyers. Consequently, they are pushed to make rash and short-term decisions based on emotional responses that do not really take into consideration the best interests of all parties in the long term.

The subsequent "bad divorces" hurt all parties involved, including the children. These bad divorces can indeed be too costly. Failing to wisely plan for your future will ultimately inflict mental and emotional scars on you, on your ex-spouse and most especially, on your children.

The subsequent chapters aim to help you go through the different stages of your divorce so you can prevent this from happening to you and your children. You still have the power to make the best out of your difficult situation as long as you recognize that you alone are responsible for your own life.

Chapter 2

Take a Brighter Perspective

I will not try to convince you that your divorce will be easy. I will be honest and tell you that it will really be hard. It can happen that you have spent the last few years struggling to make your marriage work. You finally exposed the deceptions and the half-truths that plagued your marriage. There will even be times when you will be tempted to make excuses for those half-truths and deceptions. You relentlessly try to ignore the concerned questions from your friends and family. And even if you did not really want to do it, you finally accepted the truth that you and your spouse have to go your separate ways. There are times when divorce is the best option you have.

As discussed in the previous chapter, it is inevitable for you to go through all the negative emotions that come with divorce – fear, anxiety, guilt, shame, anger and desperation. After receiving the final divorce papers, it is natural that you will feel a sudden rush of all those feelings. It is alright to be afraid. It is a big change. The future seems unclear. However, you always have the choice to look at your divorce from a brighter point of view. You are now free from a marriage that has no love and happiness. Now, you are free to take care of yourself and create a brand new life.

You can now be happier.

A lot of divorced people share the same fear that they are doomed to live the rest of their lives alone; but know that this is not true. Whatever you may be going through now, all those negative feelings will be over soon. When you are ready, you will realize that there are still a lot of things you can be thankful for. You will now have the time to do all the things you have always wanted to do. You are no longer imprisoned by your unhappy marriage. You can even start creating a friendlier relationship with your ex-spouse and a more loving bond with your children. Learn to love yourself and be happy on your own. Eventually, you will attract the right person for you – someone who can love you for who you truly are. But right, focus your attention on being happy and loving yourself.

Experts have always said that marriage can help in boosting a person's health. That cannot be true when you are trapped in an unhappy marriage. Sometimes, people tend to believe that being married, whether happily or unhappily is always better than being single. Since all of our friends are married, we do not want to be left out so we hold on to a miserable marriage. We sometimes forget that it is not really about being married but about having a happy and loving marriage. When you finally accept divorce as the best solution, you can start taking care of yourself so you will be healthy enough to do the things that are important to you and to take care of your loved ones who bring love and happiness to your life.

After your divorce, you can start to discover who you truly are. Your life will be all about you. If ever you felt lost in your marriage or you have tied up your identity with your husband or wife, you will now have the chance to know who you really want to become and the kind of life you want for yourself. You can start attending the concerts that you have always looked forward to. You can read all the books that are left unread on your bedside table. You can finally schedule your trip to Europe. Perhaps you have always wanted to take yoga or join a spin class. You can even learn a new language.

Your divorce can also help you discover how strong you really are and what you are really made of. Only the strong can successfully overcome a divorce. It takes a lot of strength and courage to confront the challenges and stress that come with the divorce process. Even the strongest and most optimistic people can feel stressed out and overwhelmed as they face and get over each of the negative emotions. Just always keep in mind that you will be able to survive. After everything is through, you will start to thrive again.

Your divorce also offers you a new chance to begin with a clean slate. You can do whatever you want in your new life. You literally own your future and you alone have the power to create the kind of life you want for yourself. You will also have the freedom to create the kind of life you want with people you choose to be with. You can go anywhere your heart desires. When all the shame and guilt are gone, you will find the energy to explore interests, events, hobbies and people that you were not able to explore when you were still married. When you are feeling depressed, you can pick yourself up by starting to dream about how you want your new life to become. Get up and start working to make your dreams come true.

Letting go of the past will allow more positive energy to enter your life so you can once again feel true happiness and joy. It is highly likely that your divorce dragged on for months or even years. During those long days, you have been living in a toxic situation. Letting go of your excess baggage will enable you turn your face towards the light and build an environment filled with positive energy.

You will have more time to focus your attention on yourself, your children, your work and your friends. You may already be aware that all of the negative energy that burdened your marriage took up most of your time – time to worry about it, talk about it, deal with it, and even lose sleep over it. Now that that toxic situation is gone, you will discover that you have a lot more free time to repurpose into devoting more time with the people you love and who love you back, including yourself.

Your blessings after your divorce will include the chance to peel off all the layers you have put on during your marriage so you can uncover all the amazing things that lie within you.

No one really enters marriage with the intention to ultimately get a divorce. But your positive expectation and right attitude can help you turn your situation into a more positive and thriving one. Hang in there. Know that once the ugly stuff is over, the good things will start to pour in.

Linda Stark

Chapter 3

Find Power in Forgiveness

Even after you have worked out the custody of your children, split your assets, sold the house and obtained a small glimmer of hope for a brighter future, your divorce process is not yet over. A lot of people who have been recently divorced focus their attention on moving on with their lives, working out how to be single once more and adapting to the changes. Many of them disregard one vital aspect of the recovery process, which is forgiveness.

The idea of forgiveness can be quite baffling for a lot of people. You may think that forgiveness means letting your spouse off the hook. You take the hit of the hurts and pain while your spouse who hurt you is now happily moving on. You may ask the question: "What if I forgive my husband and he does it again?"

You may struggle with forgiveness when you start thinking that it is not fair.

It is really difficult when your spouse who you loved with all your heart hurt you. Your wedding was wonderful. You made promises to each other, you declared your vows in front of everybody and you had great plans for a life together. Then, over the course of time, your marriage starts to weaken in both small and big heartbreaks. As your relationship deteriorates, you and your spouse find it harder and harder to forgive and forget. When you feel powerless, slighted or misunderstood, you may hold on to your anger and resentment because you do not know how you can make your spouse acknowledge or understand the pain and hurts that you are going through.

The real danger happens when you continue holding on to the pain and hurt. You continue to relive slights and insults in your head. You constantly remind yourself and other people how selfish, insensitive and hurtful your ex-spouse was. You try your very best to start feeling good and move on but you catch yourself reliving something that occurred months or years ago, and then you start to feel horrible again.

What you need to realize is that your brain cannot really differentiate between something that is actually occurring and something that you imagine is occurring. This is the reason why we get so scared while watching a scary movie and still get angry at something that occurred years ago. When you revive heartbreaks through conversation or in your head, your body and brain react as if that stress and pain were occurring right now. Allowing yourself to go through that stress all the time can damage your emotions, your body and even your future.

You can avoid causing more pain and stress by learning how to forgive. You need to recognize that forgiveness does not happen overnight, but you can begin by keeping your mind on your own thoughts since your thoughts greatly impact your moods and emotions. Make the effort to soften the edges of your thoughts associated to your ex-spouse. Yes, your ex-husband or ex-wife committed mistakes, but they definitely have good qualities that made you decide to marry them. Allow yourself to reminisce some of the tender and kind moments that that two of you once shared. Allow yourself to recognize the idea that your ex-spouse also experienced feelings of loneliness, rejection and hurt when your marriage ended.

A lot of people are afraid of doing this because they believe that reminiscing the good times will make it harder to let go of the past. What they do not understand is that the opposite is true. You can only move forward with balance in your heart and mind if you have a balanced view of your marriage and your ex-spouse. If you still recycle the old marriage moments or the same arguments again and again in your head, you may need to spend some time understanding why. What does the specific memory mean to you? Was it the exact moment when you were certain that your marriage had ended? What is the time when you recognized that you no longer felt emotionally safe with your ex-spouse? What do you think was incomplete within you that could be linked to that specific moment?

You will have to go beyond the comfort of your negative emotions and the anger of the memory. If you have to, do not hesitate to work with a relationship coach or a therapist to discover how you can access and process your deeper feelings so that you will be able to move on and build a better life.

After you have forgiven your spouse, it is also important for you to forgive your own self for all the wrong judgments and decisions that you made in the past. You need to accept that you are human and you are not perfect. You, too, are allowed to make mistakes. The important thing is for you to learn from the lessons of the past without beating yourself up. Be kind and gentle to yourself. Let go of your negative thoughts that your marriage failed or you failed. Instead, remember the blessings that you now enjoy and all the lessons you have learned during and after your marriage.

It is also helpful for you to explore any spiritual or religious beliefs that may be preventing you to forgive. Take full advantage of the second chance that you now have.

Linda Stark

Chapter 4

Take Care of Yourself

Divorce and all the subsequent changes can bring both physical and emotional stress. This is the reason why it is vital for you to ensure that your habits help you lessen the stress of divorce. By adhering to proper self-care habits, you can come out of your divorce without causing unnecessary stress to your mind and body.

Regularly visit your doctor.

Do not forget your regular visits to the doctor. See your doctor immediately if you are feeling sick so he or she can give you proper treatment to cut your recovery time. It is important that you do not place your physical well-being at the bottom of your priority list. Keep in mind that the stress that you are going through during the divorce process can cause fatigue and physical illness.

Take vitamins.

Ask your doctor to suggest vitamins and other supplements that you can take to aid your body in dealing with the extra stress.

Get regular exercise.

It is ideal to ask your doctor what specific exercises are appropriate for you and one that you can do on a regular basis. Swimming, cycling or walking are particularly good options since you will also be able to enjoy the outdoors while exercising. All other aerobic activities can help you in relieving your stress.

Do not begin any new bad habits.

Because of all the negative emotions that you are going through, you may sometimes feel tempted to smoke, drink or take recreational drugs. Remember that your difficult situation is only temporary so do not give in to the temptation. As it is, you are dealing with a lot of issues and problems surrounding your divorce so do not add to it. You wouldn't want to deal with a possible addiction when your divorce is over.

Get sufficient sleep.

Sufficient rest and sleep can give you the strength to better deal with all the changes happening in your life. If you are experiencing insomnia, it helps to keep your bedroom dark and with cool temperature. If you need new pillows, go and get them. Do not watch disturbing movies or TV programs before going to sleep. Do no exercise late at night. Taking a hot bath before going to bed can also help you relax. Do not hesitate to consult your doctor and ask about sleep aid if your sleep problems persist.

Eat a healthy diet.

Do not forget to eat. You may think that this is an obvious thing. However, it is quite easy to forget and be stressed out that you start missing breakfast, lunch or even dinner. It is vital for you to regularly eat healthy food. Make sure that you have wholesome snacks readily available so you can avoid eating junk food when you get hungry. Drink lots of juice or water. Good nutrition can also help in giving you physical strength to resist the negative effects of stress.

Learn how to let off steam.

If you are feeling angry or anxious, it is ideal for you to look for a safe way to let off steam. If you have to, purchase a punching bag. If you are concerned about the neighbors, scream into a pillow.

Cry as long as you want to. Just do not hold your anger within you to prevent it from turning into depression.

Change your scenery.

Do something to transform your environment. Buy new curtains, try painting with a new color, move your furniture around the house. After your divorce, you have all the freedom to transform your surroundings. If you do not trust your interior designing skills, you can simply opt to go outside your house and commune with nature. Go to a park, relax and simply watch the kids play. Go to a museum or an art gallery. Allow the new environment to relieve your stress.

Practice good hygiene.

Change your clothes regularly. Don't forget your regular haircuts. Take a shower every day. Visit your dentist. You may think that all these are common sense but people actually neglect to take care of themselves while going through the stressful process of divorce. When you start neglecting hygiene, it can ultimately lead to depression or physical illness.

Chapter 5

Let Go of Your Divorce Guilt

As you have learned in Chapter 1, guilt and shame are two of the strong emotions you need to overcome during your recovery process. You may continue to blame yourself for the failure of your marriage and for neglecting your children during the difficult time when you are making sense of everything that is happening to you. When you go through divorce, you may become awfully self-absorbed as you find your way through all the mess. You can be so preoccupied by your personal problems and bitterness that you neglect your children and your family and friends. It is also possible that you may be going through some financial troubles that you are not able to give more to your loved ones.

What you may not realize is that your loved ones understand you more than you think. They know the struggles that you are going through and they want to help you with whatever they can.

However, you will not be able to see that if you cannot forgive yourself for the breakup of your family. You will not be able to become truly happy again if you constantly beat yourself up for the damage that you have caused your children. You will just be further perpetuating the pain if you are not able to forgive yourself. Your shame will keep you imprisoned in a distant place, shutting everyone you love out.

After your struggles with divorce, you may end up with low self-esteem which keeps you trapped in an unworthy, guilty place. You may find it hard to believe that you are entitled to other people's forgiveness, even if you make sincere efforts to address your wrongdoings and the other person is finally willing to let go of the past. You may find it hard to believe that you could be loved for who you are. You need to keep in mind that your worth as a person is not gauged by your financial success. What you give from your heart is a lot more important.

We all make mistakes at one point or another. The great news is that we learn a lot from our failings and disappointments. When you accept your responsibility for hurting other people and try to amend your wrongdoings, you are contributing to the healing process of everyone involved. There are critical steps you need to take to release all your regrets and self-loathing. You can build a more mutual and responsive relationship with your loved ones if you give other people the chance to openly talk about the pain and remain devoted to supporting them moving forward.

The guilt that you feel now is an essential standard that can aid in clarifying your moral compass so you can remain on track and behave in ways that you feel good about. That guilt is truly healthy for you since it can guide you to conduct yourself in ways that are socially acceptable and curb your impulse to act out in ways that can result to terrible negative consequences.

Extreme guilt can paralyze you and keep you trapped in an immobilized and negative place. While your guilt can become a catalyst to center your behavior, the shame that you feel basically highlights the things you believe are wrong in yourself. The sad news is that your shame may cause you to turn inward and start loathing yourself, which can then strip you of tools that will allow you to hold onto the hope that your life will eventually become better. That shame could also make you believe that you are not worthy of other people's acceptance and love.

The irony is that as you hold on to your guilt, it will further intensify all the pains and hurt that you feel because you may retreat to a shut-off, ashamed place. This can further deny your loved ones the consideration and warmth moving forward. If you take steps to forgive yourself, you will find the strength to stand tall and reach out to your children and your family and friends in a more loving way.

Chapter 6

Find New Meaning in Your Life

The entire divorce process can seem like an emotional roller coaster ride that you would not want to ride on your own. If you have been married to your ex-spouse for a lot of years, you may find it difficult to live "out of the habit" of being married and adjust to becoming single once more.

In order to move forward in your life, you need to begin by concentrating on yourself. This is your chance to rediscover who you truly are. You can see this opportunity as a great adventure in exploring the real you.

Cherish your own magnificence.

It is really difficult for a lot of people to believe that they are born with their own magnificence. Now that you are free from an unhappy marriage, you can start thinking about how wonderful you truly are. During your marriage, you may have been thinking only of what you do not like about your life or yourself, and you may have forgotten your unique gifts. Now, you have all the time to remember. Beginning today, set a new intention to write down all your wonderful qualities and gifts such as intelligent, caring, loving, generous, kind, beautiful smile, and the list can go on. Commit to read that list on a daily basis. Continue reading the list until you truly believe what you have written. When you begin concentrating on your magnificent qualities, you will be amazed to discover that your list can be endless. Let yourself rediscover the real you. It has already been within you and now, you can let it shine.

Give yourself 10 minutes every day.

With all the negative feelings that you are going through, you may feel the need to keep yourself busy so you can keep you mind off all your worries and problems. You will only be able to be the best person you can be not only for yourself but for your kids, as well, if you allow yourself at least ten minutes every day to do something special for yourself. It can be as simple as reading a book while drinking a cup of coffee or taking a walk in the park. Always remember that when you are happy, you can make other people happy, too.

Loosen up.

When you are divorced, you can expect to have more responsibilities. This is especially true if you are now a single parent to your children or you are now responsible for certain tasks that you used to share with your ex-spouse. With these added responsibilities, you can end up completely stressed out. You can prevent this by learning to laugh more, particularly at your own self. Lighten up and learn to not take life so seriously and let things go.

Learn how to be more mindful and live in the present moment. Keep in mind that all the "good stuff" in life occurs when you live in the present. The worries of yesterday are gone forever and the to-do list of tomorrow will always be there and it can wait. When you miss this exact moment in time, you are missing out on your own life.

When you feel tense, immediately take off your blinders and leave the thoughts lurking in your head. Yes, you have the same blinders that horses wear that prevent them from seeing from side to side. It is just that your blinders are not tangible because it is all in your mind. Begin looking around you and closely observe all the things that surround you. Truly concentrate. It is ideal if you can utilize your five senses. One good example is when you are with your kids. Observe how they play. Relish their smiles. Go to them and hug them tight. Appreciate your children for being a part of your life and push yourself to see the real beauty of who your children are. You will be amazed to discover that your tension will start to diminish as a sense of peace engulfs you.

Know what truly makes you happy.

Identifying your real purpose in life can offer you a real sense of who you truly are. You will also know how you are supposed to give value to the world. It will guide your life so you can make easy and clear decisions that concern your purpose. You can think of your purpose as your compass.

When you do not know your purpose, you will end up spending your life drifting ceaselessly in whatever path life leads you. Your circumstances in life will decide for you. In the end, you will have nothing but shame, guilt, and regrets.

When you start living your life founded on your unique purpose, you will be able to live in integrity with yourself. All aspects of your life – your mind, body and soul – will be aligned to who your true self. After your divorce, use the time to concentrate on what truly matters to you. Allow yourself to experience your true passions and what your heart truly desires.

Be mindful of your thoughts and vibes.

You may have already heard of the Law of Attraction which states that "the more attention you give to something, the more attention it will give to you" or "what you think about, you bring about". After your divorce is final, it is the best time to reconnect to your own inner awareness. Learn how you can be totally still so you can fathom all the emotions that you are experiencing.

The first step is to check in with yourself to determine whether your emotions are of positive (high) energy or of negative (low) energy. Compassion, love, happiness, abundance, joy are some examples of positive energy that can aid you in moving forward in your life. A sense of lack (lack of money or time), resentment, fear and stress are examples of negative energy that can keep you trapped in the past.

When you have emotions of low energy, you can easily move towards high energy through gratitude. Be grateful for all the blessings that you have. Be thankful for all the things that are currently working in your life. When you focus your mind on the positive, you will instantly shift to a more positive energy.

Be true to yourself.

You may now be filled with a lot of doubts. You may question yourself about how you feel, what to do and what is right. You may not trust yourself to make good decisions because of how your marriage ended in failure.

When you experience this, listen to your heart. It will tell you what feels right. It will alert you when something does not feel quite right. If your heart tells you that something doesn't feel right, respect the resistance by waiting or pausing. There are times when waiting is the best option. When you wait, you are allowing the situation to evolve more easily without the need to worry.

If you feel that a particular decision is right, it generally means that you are going towards the right direction. When you learn to listen to your heart, you will be in integrity with yourself. When you are in integrity with yourself, you will know how to say "no" more effortlessly. You would not have to say yes to things which you know you will only regret.

You can prevent this from happening to you. When you catch yourself ready to say yes even when you want to say no, stop yourself. Take a deep breath. Then simply thank the other person for thinking of you but tell him that you first need to check your schedule and will get back to him. Use that extra time to know how you really feel about the request. Do you feel some resistance or are you excited to do it? If you still feel doubtful after a couple of days, perhaps it is not the right time for you to do it. If you can sense the excitement, go ahead and say yes.

There will be times when you will not be able to sleep at night or become distracted from your daily routine because of all your worries and doubt. You will wonder if you will always be plagued by your loneliness. There will be days when you will feel stuck no matter how hard you try to move forward. You will feel like you do not really know how you want your new life to turn out. Even though there are opportunities in your career or personal life, you may constantly doubt yourself. You are not even sure if you can ever date again. You may be afraid that your next relationship will be a failure again.

When you are burdened by these worries and concerns, do not wait until your life gets back on track. Do not rely on pure luck to bring happiness and love back to your life again. Pick yourself up and start planning for action. It will be hard to do it all on your own so open yourself up and seek love and support from all the people who love you and want you to be happy.

Linda Stark

Bonus Chapter

Seven Tips on How to be Emotionally Healthy

A lot of us are more mindful of our physical well-being than our emotional health. When we feel like we are about to get sick, we make sure that we are dressed warm enough. We immediately apply balms and dress our scrapes and cuts. What we do not often realize is that we also suffer from psychological injuries as much as we experience physical injuries. But the sad truth is that we are not as proactive in safeguarding our emotional health.

You can become more emotionally healthy by following the seven tips below:

Tip #1: Immediately take control after each failure.

Your perceptions can definitely become distorted after failing. You may think that you do not have the ability to accomplish the tasks you set out to do. You may also start believing that your goals are unattainable. When you allow these thoughts to get the better of you, you can find yourself demotivated and demoralized to pursue your goals. As such, it is important for you to learn how to ignore those deceptive thoughts. Instead of wallowing, you can start listing down all the things you can do to become successful in your next attempt. Do you need to take more time in planning and preparation? Are there other approaches you can take? Do you need to exert more effort? When you focus on the things that you can actually do, you will be able to win over your pessimist misperceptions. This can then significantly increase your chances of becoming successful in the future.

Tip #2: Look for meaning in trauma and loss.

One distinction between those who succeed after going through trauma or loss and those who fail is in how they look for meaning in their bad experiences. But you need to understand that finding meaning in your negative experiences does not always happen overnight. Most of the time, you will have to go through the grieving process and learn how to adapt to your new realities. But it is important that you create the habit of looking for ways to identify not only the things that you have lost but also the things that you have gained. This will let you create new appreciation for the people in your life and your life, in general.

Tip #3: Stop your urge to mull over and brood.

Brooding over disturbing events in your life does not really help in gaining insight into those negative situations. When you do so, you are only replaying enraging or hurtful scenarios in your head. This will then make you want to brood more while feeling worse. As such, you need to learn how to disrupt your brooding cycle once you notice that you are pondering over negative events in the past. Some of the things you can do include watching something you are really interested in, working on a project that you have always wanted to start on or even answering a crossword puzzle.

Tip #4: Develop your self-esteem.

It is natural for your self-esteem to fluctuate. There will be days when you feel good about yourself and there will be other days when you feel so down no matter what you do. We all go through this. But what you need to avoid is becoming too self-critical when you are going through a bad day. Do you find yourself berating yourself more when you are already feeling miserable? You can change this by viewing your self-esteem similar to how you view your physical immune system. When your self-esteem is ailing, you need to nurture it back to health. You can do this by practicing self-compassion. When you are tempted to criticize yourself, think of what you would rather say to a close friend who is going through the same situation. I am sure you will not say nasty things to a friend who is already feeling down. Learn to be as compassionate to your own self.

Tip #5: Quickly regain your self-worth after being rejected.

It is really hurtful to be rejected. You may find yourself looking for your own faults as you attempt to make sense of the hurt that you are going through. You may start to think that you are unlovable, fragile, unworthy, a loser, pathetic or weak. But keep in mind that the pain that you are feeling does not mean that there is something wrong with you. It is just how the human brain is wired. When you are going through emotional pain after a rejection, affirm all the things you value in yourself (such as a strong work ethic, creativity, compassion and loyalty). Focus on a couple of those positive qualities and think about them until you no longer feel the pain.

Tip #6: Fight loneliness by recognizing your behaviors that are self-defeating.

When you are feeling lonely, it is but natural for you to act in such a way that will lessen your risks of being rejected or frowned upon. This can then lead you to unconsciously engage in behaviors that are self-defeating and to sabotage your chances of deepening your existing relationships or creating new ones. You need to identify and challenge those self-defeating behaviors in order for you to fight your loneliness. Identify all the excuses you use in avoiding social situations and see how silly they really are. Then identify the people you truly enjoy spending time with. The next step is to commit to reaching out to a couple of those people every day to initiate plans to go out or spend time with. Do not stop until your calendar is completely filled. When you find yourself making excuses again, look for ways to challenge those excuses so you will find the courage to push through with your plans.

Tip #7: Repair your damaged relationships in order to shed your excessive guilt.

One vital factor in making your apologies effective is empathy. You will have higher chances of being forgiven by expressing a genuine apology when you have done something wrong. You need to let the other person know that you completely understand how your actions have hurt them. When the other person senses your sincerity, they will find it easier to give you their genuine forgiveness, which can then dissolve your own guilt.

Linda Stark

Bonus Chapter

Keep the Fire Alive: Building Trust through Sex

When you spend less time focusing your energy on your jealousy and on how to keep your partner from getting stolen by others, you will find that you will actually have more time to focus on how to make your next relationship even more exciting. Focus on getting to know your partner more, especially their interests and what turns them on. Intimacy in sex brings two people so much closer to each other, for such a connection is unique in that it can never be experienced elsewhere.

Take Charge of Your Thoughts and Actions:

- Spend time to gaze into your partner's eyes before you move on to physical intimacy. Get to know them more deeply simply based on how they communicate through the eyes. A powerful connection can be built between the two of you when you both can communicate with your eyes.

- You and your partner are both the lucky ones to have each other with which to experiment with different sex positions. Bond over learning about all sorts of different sex positions ever made and try out the ones that you both feel comfortable with. Let it be both a fun and a sensual experience.

- Surprise your partner by learning how to make out more intimately. Alternate between fast and slow, and soft and hard. Have fun and play around a bit by holding back for a while before going back into it. Of course, they will certainly appreciate soft lips and fresh breath, so before you pucker up make sure to brush those pearly whites and swipe on some lip balm.

- You would be surprised to know that one of the most pleasurable parts in sexual intimacy is the teasing. This is the reason why you should hold out for as long as you can during foreplay. Let the excitement build up by trying different ways to excited your partner, such as a striptease or a lap dance.

- Always leave room for surprises. Keep your partner guessing as to what would happen next in the bedroom by not limiting yourself in it! Make oh-so-hot memories in other parts of your home. Your partner will find it difficult to keep you out of their mind that way! Try to be wary of nosy neighbors, though.

- Learn to let go of your inhibitions and body image. Both of you may have your own secret body insecurities, but sex should be so much more than that. Concentrate on how you can please your partner instead, and take pleasure in their touch as well. Of course, you can always take good care of your body by eating right and working out daily if you wish.

Always remind yourselves that you should never be afraid to have fun and experiment in the bedroom. It does not matter how long you have been together, because couples often end up surprising themselves by discovering new ways to please each other and connect emotionally and physically. Do not be afraid to whip out and try those daring moves in that *kama sutra* manual that you have in the deepest part of your closet. Let loose and go wild!

Linda Stark

Conclusion

Thank you again for downloading this book!

The next step is to apply the things you have read in this book.

Finally, if you enjoyed this book, then I'd like to ask you for a favor, would you be kind enough to leave a review for this book on Amazon? I want to reach as many people as possible with this book, and more reviews will help me accomplish that. I want to help people live the best life possible.

Linda Stark

Made in the USA
San Bernardino, CA
03 August 2016